Trees
of the Cou[

Elisabeth Trotignon

Illustrations
Frédérique Schwebel
Claire Felloni
and
Catherine Lachaux
Dominique Mansion
Fernand Mognetti
Jean-Philippe Chabot

Translated by
Jo Weightman

HarperCollins*Publishers*

COLLINS WATCH GUIDES

Black and white artwork: Alban Larousse
Translation: Jo Weightman

ISBN 0 00 220101 1
© Éditions Gallimard, Paris, 1995
© in this translation HarperCollins*Publishers*, London, 1997
Printed and bound in Italy

Contents

Natural Habitats	4
Trees in the Landscape	6
Identifying Trees	8
Large Oaks	10
Holm Oak and Cork Oak	12
Beech and Birch	14
Lowland Conifers	16
Mountain Conifers	18
Mediterranean Conifers	20
Poplars	22
Willows and Alder	24
Hornbeam and Elm	26
Ash and Maple	28
Whitebeams and Fruit Trees	30
Walnut and Chestnut Trees	32
Trees in Towns	34
Yew and Cypress	36
How a Tree Works	38
Reproduction and Growth	40
The History of Trees	42
Problems Facing Trees	44
Glossary	46
Further Reading	47
Index	48

Natural Habitats

A tree does not take root at random: successful growth depends on temperature and humidity, the nature of the soil and underlying geology, relief, surrounding vegetation, etc. These factors together create a habitat to which a tree can or cannot adapt, depending on its own biological needs.

● **Beech/fir forests** often face north.

In the Mediterranean area between 400 and 100m, mountains are colonised by oak and sweet chestnut. Above that height, damp slopes support beech and dry slopes support conifers.

The sub-alpine zone is characterised by conifers (Arolla pine, mountain pine and larch)

Beech and fir are the dominant trees in the lower mountain zone between 600 and 1600m

Mediterranean seaboard

Mediterranean hill zone with low rainfall: holm oak, cork oak, Aleppo pine and stone pine are surrounded by tough, low-growing shrubs.

- Above a certain height, rainfall increases, cold intensifies and the winds grow stronger. Species which grow in the mountains are adapted to these conditions.

- Thin, dry, calcareous soils suit evergreen oaks, box, juniper and other low-growing trees and shrubs.

- Climate and relief shape the countryside: fields with hedgerows and scattered trees are found in areas of high rainfall and on rolling hills with many streams.

- In areas with a temperate climate, trees change dramatically in appearance from season to season. This does not happen in tropical regions.

In the hills on the Atlantic seaboard (0–600m) and further inland, farmers have cut down the forests and have cultivated the land to create a landscape of meadows with hedges and scattered trees

Atlantic seaboard

- A Scots pine plantation in the lowlands. Conifers, which grow more quickly and produce more timber than broad-leaved trees, have been the preferred choice for reafforestation since the 19th century. The trend nowadays is to return to planting broad-leaved trees.

- Local conditions also affect the life of trees: the pattern of light and shade may be critical or a strong wind may twist trees and cause stunted growth.

Trees in the Landscape

Trees are the living part of a landscape. Whether they have been planted for economic or aesthetic reasons, or whether they have regenerated naturally on abandoned plots, trees with their irregular bulk and outline which changes as the seasons and years go by, give character to a site. Living, but vulnerable too: a storm, or people, may suddenly remove them and dramatically change the landscape.

● On flat, open land or in the middle of a field, an **isolated tree** may form a landscape all by itself: it forms a landmark and lends scale. The seasons are marked by its changing leaf colour and the bare branches in winter.

● A **patchwork** of fields, hedges and trees owes everything to people. Hedges are both beautiful and useful: a windbreak, boundary, a source of timber and shelter for wildlife.

● **Fruit trees**, standing in a meadow or on a hillside, bring colour to the landscape, brightening it with blossom in spring and with splashes of red and green from leaves and fruit in summer.

Conifers

● Conifers can be easily distinguished from broad-leaved trees by their outline. The latter usually have a rounded or oval shape while conifers are normally pyramidal or triangular.

Common silver fir
Short needles with a rounded tip, parted and spreading either side of the shoot

Thuja
Shoots flattened, leaves closely appressed, scale-like

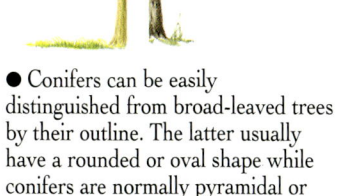

Scots pine
Rather short, twisted needles in pairs

Maritime pine
Long, rigid needles in pairs

Mountain pine
Rather short, thick needles in pairs

Aleppo pine
Needles gathered in a tuft at the end of the shoot, in pairs

Stone (umbrella) pine
Long, fairly rigid needles in pairs

Austrian pine
Stiff needles in pairs

Lawson cypress
Leaves flat, scale-like, closely appressed

Common yew
Flat, pointed leaves with very short petioles

Larch
Soft needles arranged in tufts on the old wood

Norway spruce
Short needles arranged spirally on the shoot

Scots pine
All pines have needles that are more or less long and slender and mostly grouped in pairs

Cedar
Cedar needles are short and stiff, arranged singly on the shoot or in small tufts

Common yew
The short, flat, supple leaves of the common yew are arranged in two ranks

Cypress
The cypress has tiny, scale-like needles very closely appressed to the shoot

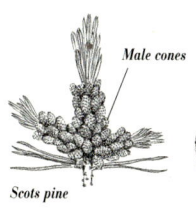

Scots pine (Male cones)
Conifers have separate male and female flowers or cones. The male cone of the Scots pine is yellow.

Scots pine
After fertilisation, the female flower develops into a cone from which the seeds escape when ripe

Young cedar
The cedar has a cylindrical cone with a flattened top. Its scales are greenish when young.

Cedar, ripe cone
After two years, when it is ripe, the cone is purplish. It disintegrates on the tree, leaving only its central column behind

Scots pine
The Scots pine cone is long and green when young: after a year it turns brown and the scales open

The cone of the common silver fir (left) stands erect on the shoot: the spruce cone (right) hangs down

Common yew
The fruit of the yew is not a cone. A red fleshy aril surrounds the very poisonous seed.

Cypress
Cypress fruits are small round cones bearing a few stalked scales

● The soil in **conifer woods** is poor: the fallen leathery needles, full of resin, are not attractive to worms. A thick litter builds up forming a black, acid layer incapable of supporting many flowering plants.

- **A row of trees** lining the banks of a canal form a gentle landscape. They make a road or canal into a work of art.

- **Woodlands** form remarkable landscapes varying in appearance with the seasons and the time of day.

- Trees are everywhere **in towns**: in parks, along roads and in courtyards.

Plane tree

Identifying Trees

Thuja

Common silver fir

Maritime pine

Scots pine

Some trees can be identified from their shape alone, but flowers, fruits, buds, branches and the shape and position of the leaves can all help to identify a tree. Bark also has very useful diagnostic characters. However, it is important to bear in mind that, when young, the colour of bark is not distinctive, and it is often smooth, tending to develop deep cracks only when it gets older.

Austrian pine

Stone (umbrella) pine

Aleppo pine

Mountain pine

Norway spruce

Larch

Common yew

Lawson cypress

Broad-leaved Trees

Oak leaf — *Blade, Vein, Rounded lobes*
Leaf sessile (joined directly to the shoot) and lobed (blade cut into lobes, rounded in this species)

Beech leaf
Leaf simple, ovate, with 6–8 pairs of rather prominent parallel veins

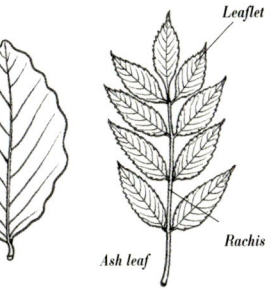

Ash leaf — *Leaflet, Rachis*
Leaf compound composed of several separate leaflets arranged in pairs on the rachis

Sycamore leaf — *Ovate toothed lobes, Sinus, Petiole*
Leaf lobed and palmate, with 5 ovate toothed lobes, separated by sinuses

Apple blossom
Crab apple flowers are arranged in groups of 4–5 at the end of the shoot

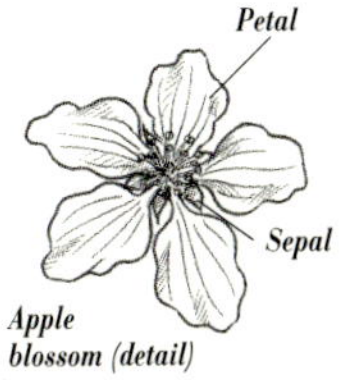

Apple blossom (detail) — *Petal, Sepal*
Flower composed of a calyx (sepals), a corolla (petals), stamens and stigma

Female willow catkin
A catkin is a number of unisexual flowers grouped in a tight cluster

Male willow catkin
Hazel, willow and poplar all have catkins. These often appear before the leaves.

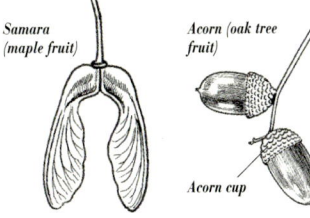

Samara (maple fruit)
A samara is a winged, dry fruit. The wings make it spin when it falls in autumn.

Acorn (oak tree fruit) — *Acorn cup*
Oak tree fruits (acorns) are often ovoid. They are borne in scaly cupules (acorn cups).

Rowan fruits
Rowans have fleshy fruits which attract birds

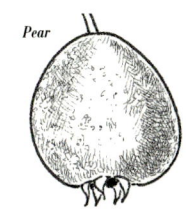

Pear
The small wild pear has tart fruit. The skin is covered in lenticels (breathing pores).

● The leaves of many **broad-leaved trees** fall to the ground in the autumn. Other plants thrive on the rotting leaves. In early spring, flowering plants can grow as light still filters through the canopy.

False acacia
Leaf compound with ovate leaflets

White poplar
Leaf simple, silvery, cottony beneath

Black walnut
Leaf compound, with lanceolate leaflets

Common walnut
Leaflets oblong, with a leathery blade

Common ash
Leaf compound, with lanceolate leaflets

Purple willow
Leaves are bluish-green and hairless with very fine teeth

Sycamore
Lobes ovate, toothed, sinus narrow, petiole long

Field maple
Leaf with five rounded leaflets, two not very pronounced

Downy birch
Leaf toothed, pubescent, triangular

Plane
Leaf palmate with triangular toothed lobes

Durmast oak
Leaf with rounded lobes, petiole long

Cork oak
Leaf simple, with a slightly inrolled, ovate blade; evergreen

Beech
Leaf simple with an ovate blade, edge wavy

Apple tree
Leaf rounded, with a pointed, finely toothed tip

Broad-leaved lime
Leaf finely pubescent

Sweet chestnut
Leaf long, lanceolate, strongly toothed

Identifying Trees

Common walnut · Black walnut · White poplar · False acacia

Field maple · Sycamore · Crack willow · Common ash

Cork oak · Durmast oak · Plane · Downy birch

Horse chestnut · Broad-leaved lime · Apple · Beech

- The **red oak** from the United States grows more quickly than its European relatives. It is used in reafforestation.

- The **Pyrenean oak** is a small tree with a twisted trunk. It grows best on the dry, acid soils of south-west Europe.

Red oak

Pedunculate oak

Acorn ovoid, cupule green, rather shallow

- The **red oak** can be recognised by its large leaves which turn orange or even an intense red in the autumn. They have pointed lobes.

Pedunculate oak: male flowers yellow, arranged in small pendulous clusters (catkins)

The fruit is borne on a long peduncle from which the tree derives its name

- The **pedunculate oak** is often planted in woodland. Unlike the sessile oak, it requires rich, damp soil and suffers badly when there is a drought.

- When growing in the open, oaks have wide, spreading branches; within a wood, they have a narrower profile.

- The **pedunculate oak** often grows on its own in parkland and in roadside hedges.

Large Oaks

Oaks, venerated by the ancient Greeks, Romans and Celts, are divided into several species. Of these, the pedunculate and durmast oaks make mighty trees. They hold the records for girth (up to 3.5m) and longevity: some are more than a thousand years old. The high quality timber is used in ship building, structural work and for very solid furniture, but it takes a good 100 years for an oak to grow large enough to cut.

Durmast oak

Distinctly petiolate leaves

Small, sessile acorns

● The **durmast oak** grows well on light or acid soils. It is also called the sessile oak because its acorns have no stalks.

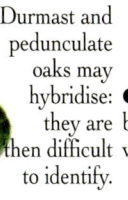

● Durmast and pedunculate oaks may hybridise: they are then difficult to identify.

● **Oak wood** is often used for making barrels. Port matures well in oak casks which have previously held wine.

The leaf of the pedunculate oak is oblong and wavy with rounded lobes. It is attached to the shoot by a very short petiole.

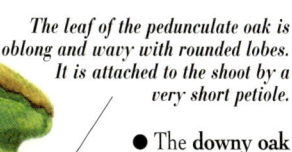

● The **downy oak** has a short, twisted trunk and dark, rough bark. The leaves are small, alternate, and pubescent beneath.

● The **downy oak** is a southern species. When growing in more northern regions, it likes rather dry, calcareous soils.

Holm Oak and Cork Oak

Holm and cork oaks are the outstanding trees of the Mediterranean region. The climate is difficult: hot dry summers with intense light, uncertain rainfall and sudden outbreaks of cold weather. These oaks therefore grow slowly, never exceeding 20m in height. The original forests suffered badly from clearance and fire: large stands are very rare today.

● **Holm oaks** are small trees with a short trunk and wide, spreading branches. They grow well when spaced apart from each other and dominate scrub rich in such plants as cistus, holly oak and sage.

Leaves ovate, dark green, glossy above, whitish and pubescent beneath

Cambium

Holm oak

Acorn fairly long

● The thick bark of the cork oak, the **cork**, is pale grey and often deeply cracked.

● These trees are adapted for dry conditions: they have leathery, waxy leaves which limit loss of water through transpiration. They are evergreen: thanks to them, woodlands in the Mediterranean remain green all year round.

● When cork is first removed, the practice is called 'unmasking'. It is done in summer when the bark can be detached easily from the trunk. Underneath is the orange-red **cambium**.

Acorns borne in a cup with velvety scales

Cork oak: leaves dark green, sometimes with sharp teeth

Strawberry tree: the fruits are edible

Holly oak: the acorn cup is covered with sharp points

Spurge

Holly oak (often grazed down to about 1m): a shrub or tree with tiny prickly leaves, often found in garrigue

● Damaged woodland is replaced by garrigue (on calcareous soils) or maquis (on acid soils). Both consist of evergreen shrubs.

Clumps of rosemary, thyme and cistus. The latter is very aromatic in spring and has the unwelcome property of helping fire spread very rapidly.

13

Beech and Birch

Beech, with oak, is supreme in European woodlands, forming splendid stands, while the humble birch is associated with damaged woodland and heathland. Both formerly played an important part in rural life.

- **Birch bark** is white and peels off in horizontal strips. It is tender and sweet in spring.

- **Beech** has spreading branches and its leaves form a dense canopy that cuts out much of the light. Few plants manage to grow under mature beeches.

- **Silver birch** occurs in all open woodland on poor soils. It is very often the first species to recolonise burnt or waste ground but disappears once taller trees are established as it cannot tolerate shade.

- In times gone by, birch bark was eaten in spring in northern Europe. It was also used to make sandals and to roof huts. It had many medicinal uses.

Silver birch

Downy birch

Leaf blunt at base, triangular, unevenly toothed

Leaf diamond-shaped, pubescent, uniformly toothed

Hairy petiole

- Birches grow very quickly at first, but do not live for more than about 100 years.

- **Downy birch** favours wet or even boggy ground, especially in northern Europe.

Leaves green, glossy, ovate, with a wavy edge, petiolate

Nuts or mast, two in each cupule

Prickly, woody cupule

Beech

- The **beech** has a smooth, straight, ash-grey trunk. Its timber is widely used to make furniture.

- Although it is widespread in Europe, the **beech** is demanding in its requirements: when young it only grows well in the shade of older trees, which it will replace as it matures. It also requires a moist atmosphere on well drained soils. Given these conditions, it will live for up to 300 years.

Scots pine: open irregular crown, bluish foliage, scaly, light reddish bark

- Woodland in the Landes in south-west France is almost entirely composed of the **maritime pine** which was planted in the 19th century to improve the region which was at that time marshy and poor.

- In northern Europe the trunk of the **Scots pine** is more or less straight. In the Mediterranean it grows at an angle and is rather curved. The tree reaches 40m and lives for 100 to 200 years.

Scots pine

Needles short and bluish-green, arranged in pairs, twisted

Scots pine cone: small and ovoid. The youngest occur on the terminal shoot while older cones occur further back along the branch.

- In the illustration below, a few birch, sweet chestnut and heather patches occur in a stand of Scots pine. All these plants like well-lit, open places and prefer rather acid soils.

Lowland Conifers

Maritime pine

The Scots pine and maritime pine are well adapted for poor soils. They make good plantation trees and in Europe today cover vast areas of land alongside introduced or mountain conifers such as the Douglas fir or spruce. However, these coniferous monocultures degrade and acidify the soil, making the habitat poor for wildlife: birds, for example, are rarer than in broad-leaved woodland.

The maritime pine has a loose, open, slightly conical crown

Maritime pine cone: ovoid, glossy brown and very large

Needles dark green, long and thick, in pairs

Douglas fir

Characteristic bracts on the cone

● The **Douglas fir** is widely planted in Europe but does not root well and cannot withstand winds.

The cone of the Douglas fir hangs from its branch. 3-pointed, leaf-like bracts fit over the scales.

Mountain Conifers

Conifers have better resistance to extreme conditions than broad-leaved trees. This is why many species are found above 1000m. But these trees do not occur at random: larch and Arolla pine prefer sunny slopes while fir and spruce are dominant on north-facing mountain sides.

● **Beech/fir woods** occur on north-facing slopes where the air is moist.

Spruce forests have a poor understorey as light levels are low

Spruce

Needles short, arranged spirally on the shoot, which looks like a bottle brush

Long, pendulous cone unlike that of the fir. It falls to the ground after the seeds have dispersed.

● The **mountain pine** is related to the Scots pine (see page 16), differing in the greyish bark and hooked scales on the cone.

Mountain pine

- The **Arolla pine** has dense foliage on its spreading, sometimes upturned, branches which are often retained to ground level. The long needles, in bundles of 5, are a dark, rather bluish-green.

Spring Summer Autumn Winter

- The **larch** is a tall tree (30–40m) with a straight trunk and pyramidal crown.

- Unlike other conifers, **larch** loses its leaves in winter. The needles, which are a tender green in spring, turn russet in autumn before falling.

Arolla pine

Small, ovoid cones with closely appressed brown scales

The soft, light green needles occur in tufts on the older wood, as shown here. They occur singly on the young wood.

- **Larch** is a tree of wood pasture. Grass grows readily beneath its light cover and mountain livestock (cows, sheep) seek its shelter.

Larch

19

- The mountains in Corsica support many pines: between 900 and 1800m, **Corsican pine** grows with beech, fir and sweet chestnut.

- **Corsican pine** likes a humid microclimate and well drained, siliceous soils.

- Like spruce, Corsican pine is used in reafforestation. Plantations cover huge areas in lowland and mountain regions, bringing impoverished land back into use, but forming a monotonous landscape.

The Calabrian pine is distinguished from the Corsican pine by its needles which are longer and finer and not twisted

Corsican pine

Cone rather small, ovoid

Needles slender, twisted, grey-green

- The **Corsican pine** has a straight trunk, bare to a considerable height. It often reaches 50m.

Corsican pine

Stone pine

Needles long, fairly stout, in pairs

- The **stone (umbrella) pine** has a very distinctive shape: the very branched crown spreads out like an umbrella over a bare trunk with deeply cracked orange-beige bark.

Scale, kernel and cone of the stone pine

- **Stone pine cones** bear large, edible seeds called kernels. They are used to decorate cakes.

Mediterranean Conifers

Poor soil, low rainfall and intense summer heat in many areas of southern Europe combine to make life very difficult for trees. But, like the cork and holm oaks, some conifers have adapted to these conditions: the Aleppo pine, which likes dry conditions, the stone pine and, higher up, the Corsican pine, occupy an important place in the Mediterranean landscape.

● The **Aleppo pine** has a distinctive, often contorted trunk rising to an irregular spreading crown which widens with age. Its height rarely exceeds 20m. It is tolerant of very dry conditions but succumbs to fire and the caterpillar of the processionary moth.

Aleppo pine

Stone pine

● The **Aleppo pine** is often the first to recolonise a site destroyed by fire or left unplanted. As it never forms a dense stand, an understorey of holly oak, cistus, rosemary and other shrubs develops.

Aleppo pine

Slender, rather yellowish needles

Cones small and ovoid, often with a strong purple sheen, remain on the branches for a long time after seed fall

Needles arranged in pairs, in brush-like tufts at the end of the branches

Poplars

Poplars like river banks and deep, damp soils. They do so well in these conditions that in the last few decades they have invaded valley areas: much peat bog, flood plain and alluvial woodland has been replaced by profitable – and often monotonous – rows of poplar trees.

- It is rather hard to tell one species of poplar from another in Europe. This is because Middle Eastern species were hybridised with North American poplars in the early 19th century.

- **Aspen**, a small poplar, prefers clearings.

Simple round leaves which tremble in the slightest breeze

Pendulous catkins, the males greyish (above), the females greenish

Black poplar

Female catkins pedunculate, yellowish, pendulous

Male catkins sessile, pendulous, becoming red-purple. Pollen is released in March.

Black poplar leaf: triangular, both surfaces green, slightly toothed, carried on a short, flattened petiole

- The **black poplar** has a wide crown and low, dense, bushy branches. In the winter, the horizontal branches can be seen.

22

- Lines of **poplars** are very prone to wind damage.

- The **white poplar** has wonderful silvery foliage and a rounded crown.

Male catkins hairy, reddish

White poplar

White poplar leaves: silvery and cottony with pronounced lobes

Lombardy poplar: leaf wider than long

- Poplars all carry their flowers in catkins. Male and female catkins are always borne on separate trees.

- **Lombardy poplar** can be recognised by its trunk which has branches almost to the base and its long, narrow profile.

Willows and Alder

Willows and alder both need to be close to water: they live on river banks where they grow in lines. They also occur in some marshy lowlands and damp woods where they form impenetrable thickets with climbing shrubs, mounds of sedge, common reeds and fallen trees.

Wavy, oblong leaves with prominent veins beneath

● Like many willows, **common sallow** (also called pussy willow) flowers open early in spring, before the leaves.

● **Willow** catkins have abundant nectar which is gathered by insects. Cottony threads around the seeds aid wind dispersal.

● Willows are difficult to identify as they hybridise with one another.

● **Common alder** often grows in association with ash or willow on river banks. When growing in the open it has a broad outline with spreading branches.

Leaf ovate, almost round, flattened at the tip, rather sticky in spring

Common alder

● **White willow** grows in damp meadows beside rivers. Once pollarded regularly, but now generally allowed to grow up unchecked.

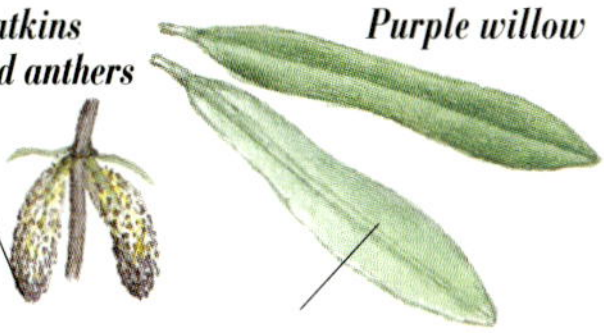

● In winter the tree can be recognised from afar by its woody fruits or **cones**. They contain seeds which are much sought after by siskins.

Male catkins with red anthers

Purple willow

Twigs purple. Leaves long, wider and toothed towards the tip.

● **Common alder** has a dense network of roots which bind the river bank securely and give the tree good wind resistance.

● As soon as it is cut, alder wood changes from white to brick-red. New growth springs up, as **coppice wood**, around the stump, which eventually dies.

● **Purple willow** does not exceed 6m. Like most other willows, it is used in basket-making.

New coppice growth

The roots, which are well anchored into the bank, form good hiding places for fish

Hornbeam and Elm

Hornbeam often branches low down in hedges and higher up in coppice woodland

In times gone by, rural communities had many uses for hornbeam and elm. Tools were made from the wood and cattle were fed with the foliage in winter. These trees are still an important feature of the rural landscape even if this economic interest has now diminished: they occur frequently in hedges, copses, on woodland edges and near buildings.

● **Hornbeam** makes an excellent hedgerow, forming a solid windbreak.

● In some areas, laid **hornbeam hedges** survive. The tree throws up new shoots from the cut base and withstands repeated cutting.

Female flowers at the tip of the shoot

Leaves dark green, ovate-lanceolate, irregularly toothed, the mid-rib prominent

Longer, hanging, male catkins

Hornbeam flowers and leaves

● Like a few other broad-leaved trees, young **hornbeam**, or hornbeam in a hedge, will retain its withered leaves for a good part of the winter.

Numerous branches, dense, almost ovoid, crown

Trunk fluted, with smooth, ash-grey bark

Hornbeam

- In many areas, **elm** was once the dominant hedgerow tree. Mature trees declined rapidly between 1970 and 1980 following attack by that mortal enemy of the elm, Dutch elm disease.

- The disappearance of the mighty elms changed the landscape. However, the species suckers freely and the saplings grow quickly – but can they outlive the disease?

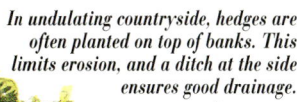

In undulating countryside, hedges are often planted on top of banks. This limits erosion, and a ditch at the side ensures good drainage.

- Like other species, **elm** can be pollarded or cut back. Every 15 to 20 years the branches are cut back to the trunk and the tree takes on a strange, even disturbing appearance. Knotted wood is much sought after for cabinet-making.

Wych elm

Large leaves, with three tips (one on each shoulder)

English elm pollards

English elm: rounded crown, rather dense, dark green foliage, massive trunk, dark brown bark with deep vertical cracks. In the open, the tree may reach 30m.

Wych elm and smooth-leaved elm fruits have a central seed

Red flowers borne near the tips of the twigs

The seed of the English elm is close to the tip of the fruit

English elm leaves are toothed and very rough

Ash and Maple

Opposite leaves with rather rounded lobes

Samara with horizontal wings

Common ash and field maple are common in Europe excluding mountainous and Mediterranean regions. As they grow rapidly, they were used for firewood and fodder, and for making a wide range of objects.

● **Field maple** is often a small tree found in hedges and woodlands.

Sycamore

Leaf large, wide, opposite

Sycamore samaras: wings at about 90 degrees, in pairs in a drooping raceme

Montpelier maple

Lobes ovate, irregularly toothed, separated by a narrow sinus

Italian maple

Long, reddish petiole

Sycamore: dense crown, foliage dark green

● **Sycamore** often reaches 35m. Seed germinates well and young growth is very rapid. It is very common near houses and along roads.

- The **common ash** prefers cool sites: riversides, damp woods, shady slopes, hedges. It does not live to a great age (200 years at most), but suckers and reproduces freely.

- Once used to build carriages, ash has since been used to make solid billiard cues and tennis rackets. A valuable timber for tool handles.

Opposite leaves with 7–15 pairs of shallowly toothed, lanceolate leaflets

Black bud

Common ash

Samara (ash keys) in bunches retained on the tree in winter

Male flowers in rounded clusters

Female flowers in longer and more open clusters

Common ash

- A southern species, the **narrow-leaved ash** requires warmth and light. It grows along watercourses or in hedgerows. It is most easily distinguished from the common ash by its purplish-brown buds.

Narrow-leaved ash: light foliage and rather rugged bark

- Ash leaves and bark are used to make refreshing tonic drinks.

● In lowland areas, whitebeams and wild cherry often grow in association with other trees – oak, lime, hornbeam, maples. On the dry, calcareous soils of lower mountain slopes, whitebeam is rather more abundant.

Whitebeams and Fruit Trees

The rose family includes numerous fruit trees, both wild and cultivated, which are popular with people, birds and even bees which feed on the nectar in the flowers. They often occur near houses, in parks and hedges or in coppice with standards.

Wild cherry

Milky-white petals, orange-red stamens

White flowers on long pedicels, in clusters, appearing before the leaves

Small, blackish-red fruit, bitter when ripe

Leaves glossy both sides, with 5–9 unequal pointed lobes

Wild service tree (autumn)

● The **wild cherry** or **gean** is the ancestor of the cultivated cherry.

Flower of the wild service tree: round, white, spreading petals

Fruit brown, with rust-coloured spots, leathery

● **Wild service** fruits, which are too bitter for humans, are much appreciated by birds.

Flowers arranged in a dense corymb

True service tree: rounded crown, straight trunk, dark bark with small scales, leaves with toothed leaflets

● Fruit trees are grown in orchards and, in some areas, in hedges.

● **True service trees**, once planted in rural areas, are now becoming rare. The fruit looks like a small pear and is eaten when over-ripe.

● Since ancient times, wild species of cherry, pear, apple etc., have been gradually improved to give the cultivated varieties we eat today.

● In autumn, many birds, such as the **song thrush**, feast on vitamin-rich wild fruit and berries.

● **Apple trees** have clusters of 4–8 white flowers, flushed pink beneath, with yellow stamens.

● The flowers of the **wild pear** are white with crimson stamens and arranged in clusters.

Crab apples: small and bitter-tasting

● Wild apples and pears are usually eaten cooked. Raw, they will keep all winter.

Wild pear: dark green, ovate leaves with a long petiole

Small, yellow-green fruits with a bitter taste. Calyx of the flower at the end of the fruit.

31

Walnut and Chestnut Trees

- The male flowers of the **common walnut** hang in thick catkins on the previous year's wood: the smaller female flowers occur at the tip of the shoots.

Male catkin

Since Roman times, the common walnut and sweet chestnut have been cultivated in southern and central Europe for their nuts, timber and other products which were used by rural communities. The horse chestnut, a 12th century introduction, is widely planted as an ornamental tree.

- **Common walnut** never grows into a large tree and rarely lives more than 200 years. It always grows in an open situation. The crown is rounded and the trunk short.

Black walnut

Common walnut

- **Common walnut**, a cultivated tree, occurs in gardens and beside roads but rarely in woodland.

Leaves with 15–25 widely spaced, lanceolate, shallowly-toothed leaflets

Leaves with 5–9 oblong, leathery leaflets, the terminal leaflet being larger. They have been used medicinally.

Leaves 10–20cm long, lanceolate, strongly-toothed, glossy above, paler beneath

Chestnut and its very prickly cupule

In the open, the rather low, heavy branches of the sweet chestnut spread widely from a straight trunk

- **Sweet chestnut**, with other trees, is grown as a windbreak. There is less call for its products today and the tree is declining. It has also suffered from diseases.

Yellow male flowers

Sweet chestnut

Leaf large, palmate, with 5-7 toothed leaflets, broader towards the tip, all inserted on a long petiole

Black walnut: a tall tree with a straight trunk and broad crown

Horse chestnut leaf

● The **horse chestnut** can have red or white flowers.

● The **black walnut** was introduced into Europe from America at the end of the 17th century.

Horse chestnut

Shuck *Shell*

Spiny case with one or two shiny, mahogany-coloured seeds, the conkers

The fruit of the common walnut is composed of a shuck, a fleshy casing which loosens from the brown woody shell when ripe. Inside is the kernel which is commonly eaten. It also yields a good edible oil.

Black walnut fruit: shell very hard to crack, kernel bitter-tasting

Trees in Towns

The cedar of Lebanon, introduced into Europe in the 17th century, has become very rare in its country of origin

Weeping willow

● The **Judas tree**, a native of the Middle East, was probably introduced into Europe at the time of the Crusades.

Trees do not just happen in towns; they are planted. Ornamental species are usually chosen for the fine colours of their leaves and flowers. Streets, parks and gardens are decked out in exotic species, never seen in the natural state in the wild here. They were brought back by explorers from the 16th century onwards.

● The **London plane** is quite tolerant of atmospheric pollution and roots down well in the hard-packed soil under pavements.

False acacia

● The **false acacia** from the United States has spread throughout temperate regions.

London plane: very large, lobed leaves, fruits 1–3 stalked, globular clusters of nutlets

Orange tree

Fragrant flowers in March, fruit during the winter

Species requiring heat are grown in greenhouses

● **Lime** is undemanding and makes an imposing tree in gardens. It has sweet-scented blossom and may live up to 1000 years.

Lime

● Botanic gardens such the Royal Botanic Gardens at Kew in Surrey, are stocked with exotic species.

● **Eucalyptus**, which was brought back from Australia by a botanist accompanying Cook, can reach 100m. It can be seen in parks.

Eucalyptus

● **Palm tree** leaves grow from the top of the trunk. There are nearly 3,000 species of palm, most of them confined to tropical areas of the world.

Yew and Cypress

Yew and cypress are conifers. As both can easily be kept in shape by cutting, they are popular with gardeners. They can be seen in gardens, near houses and in cemeteries. Yew is adapted for damp northern countries while cypress prefers the dry heat of the south.

Cypress have cones, composed of 10–14 scales

Leaves scale-like, in close ranks, evergreen

● Because of its dense foliage, cypress is often used as a windbreak around kitchen gardens.

The single seed, when ripe, has a fleshy red aril around it instead of a cone

Common yew

● **Italian cypress**, which came originally from Asia Minor, is typical of the Mediterranean landscape. It has an unmistakable pencil shape.

Leaves green, darker on the upper side, soft, shortly petiolate

Trunk often short, with many branches from the base. In the open, yew has a squat, compact appearance

● **Yew** can be cut into any shape the gardener fancies. This cutting is called topiary can be admired in many parks.

● **Yew** can often live for 1000 years. It occurs with holly and box in the moist atmosphere of the understorey beneath beech.

A tree is a plant with a large woody stem (a trunk) and branches. All trees have a certain number of features in common connected with their biological function: respiration and photosynthesis, nutrition, reproduction and growth, and also with their evolution and ecology. The leaves, fruit, bark and profile of trees vary greatly according to the species and are used in identification.

How a Tree Works

In order to live and grow, a tree needs light, oxygen, carbon dioxide, water and mineral salts. Roots, trunk and leaves all have a part to play in four life-giving processes: photosynthesis, respiration, nutrition and transpiration.

● Light and atmospheric carbon dioxide (CO_2) are essential for photosynthesis to occur. During the day, the green leaves fix the carbon (C) and give off the oxygen (O), without which we could not live.

● Like animals, trees breathe. They take in oxygen and breathe out carbon dioxide. This process, which is masked during the day by photosynthesis, is more obvious at night when there is no light for photosynthesis.

Open stoma

● A leaf has microscopic pores called **stomata** through which there is an exchange of gases, especially transpired water vapour, between the tree and the surrounding air.

● The quantity of water a tree gives off during transpiration is phenomenal: in the summer an ash tree gives off up to 200 litres per day.

● At the tips of the roots are **rootlets** with absorbant hairs which draw in the water and mineral salts which the tree requires. This forms the raw sap which is drawn right up to the leaves through tubes in the trunk and branches.

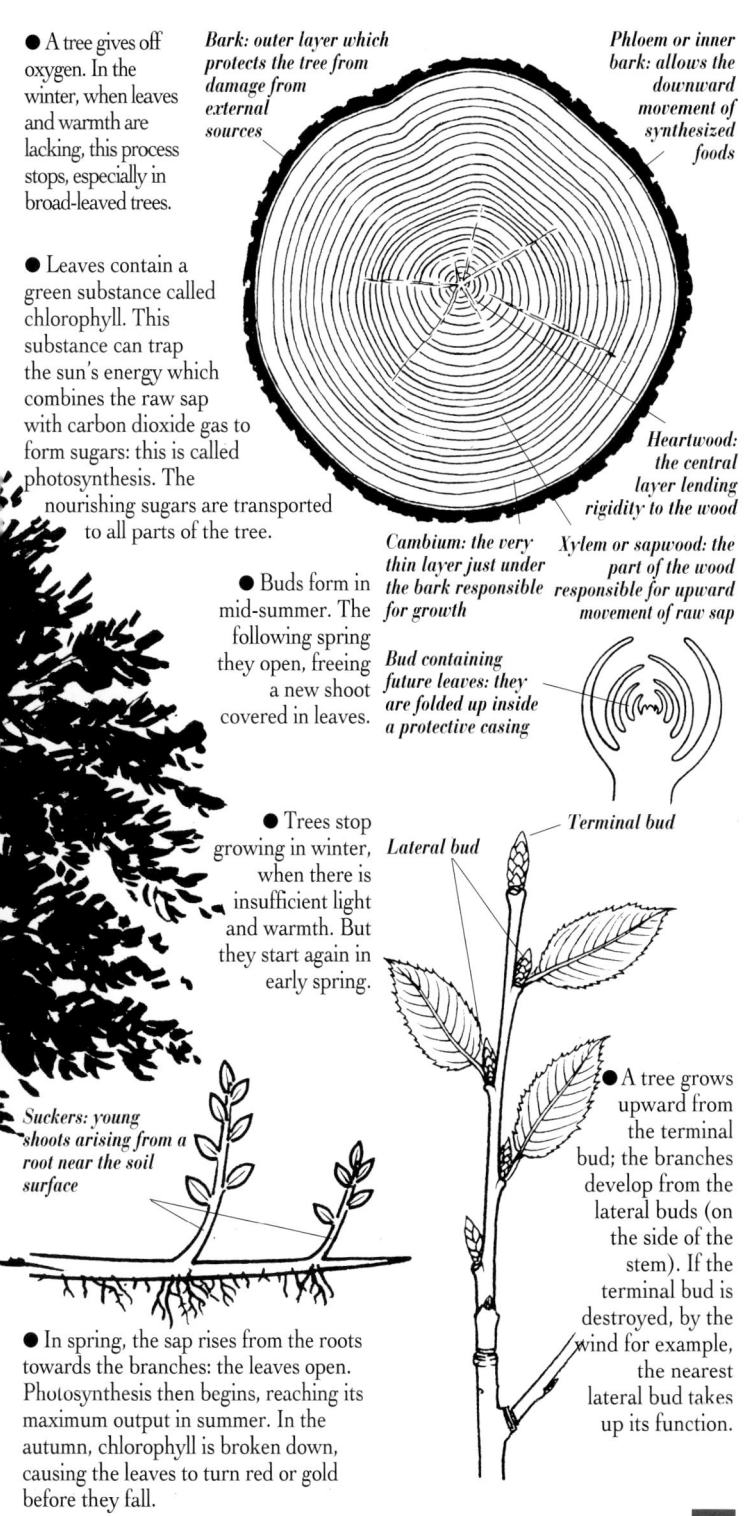

- A tree gives off oxygen. In the winter, when leaves and warmth are lacking, this process stops, especially in broad-leaved trees.

- Leaves contain a green substance called chlorophyll. This substance can trap the sun's energy which combines the raw sap with carbon dioxide gas to form sugars: this is called photosynthesis. The nourishing sugars are transported to all parts of the tree.

Bark: outer layer which protects the tree from damage from external sources

Phloem or inner bark: allows the downward movement of synthesized foods

Heartwood: the central layer lending rigidity to the wood

Cambium: the very thin layer just under the bark responsible for growth

Xylem or sapwood: the part of the wood responsible for upward movement of raw sap

- Buds form in mid-summer. The following spring they open, freeing a new shoot covered in leaves.

Bud containing future leaves: they are folded up inside a protective casing

- Trees stop growing in winter, when there is insufficient light and warmth. But they start again in early spring.

Lateral bud

Terminal bud

Suckers: young shoots arising from a root near the soil surface

- A tree grows upward from the terminal bud; the branches develop from the lateral buds (on the side of the stem). If the terminal bud is destroyed, by the wind for example, the nearest lateral bud takes up its function.

- In spring, the sap rises from the roots towards the branches: the leaves open. Photosynthesis then begins, reaching its maximum output in summer. In the autumn, chlorophyll is broken down, causing the leaves to turn red or gold before they fall.

39

Reproduction

In order for reproduction to take place, male pollen and female ovules must come together. These are often borne on the same tree, even on the same flower (as in the wild cherry, for example). But fertilisation often occurs much further away, on another tree. Nature favours cross fertilisation which ensures species vigour.

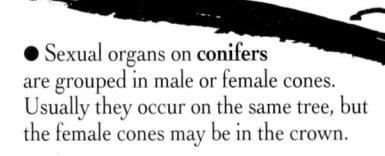

● Sexual organs on **conifers** are grouped in male or female cones. Usually they occur on the same tree, but the female cones may be in the crown.

● The flower of the **wild cherry** is composed of two protective envelopes: the brightly coloured corolla (petals) and the usually green calyx (sepals). Inside are the stamens, male organs laden with pollen, surrounding the carpel. The latter contains the ovary, the female organ enclosing the eggs.

● Broad-leaved trees are often **pollinated by insects** which brush against the pollen, and carry it to a flower on another tree. Fertilisation then takes place.

● Pollen grains can be borne on the wind and fertilise flowers on another tree: this is wind pollination.

● After fertilisation the petals fade, the ovules become seeds and the ovary develops into a fruit. Wild cherry fruits are particularly attractive to birds.

● Thanks to birds, the seeds within fruit are dispersed and give rise to seedling trees some distance from the parent.

and Growth

Old Scots pines often lose their lower branches

- Conifers are strictly wind pollinated: pollen is carried on the wind, sometimes quite a long way. A single pollen grain, coming in contact with a female flower, is sufficient for fertilisation.

Ovule-bearing scale

- A **female cone** is composed of closely-packed scales. Each scale bears naked ovules but they are well sheltered from bad weather.

When they have been fertilised, male **cones** become woody. They contain seeds which have a papery wing which assists dispersal. Once on the ground, the seeds are subjected to the cold of winter before they germinate.

Young female cones

- After seed dispersal, the **cones** distintegrate on the tree or fall to the ground.

- All seedlings do not grow to full size trees: they may be eaten by animals, lack light or water or suffer from a late frost.

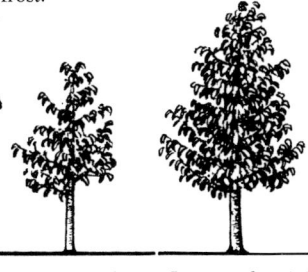

- A **young cherry** flowers when it is about 10 years old. It grows rapidly, its circumference increasing by 2.5–3cm each year for most of its life.

The History of Trees

Plant life began on earth 500 million years ago. Mosses, of aquatic origin, became established – they had stems and leaves but, as yet, no roots.

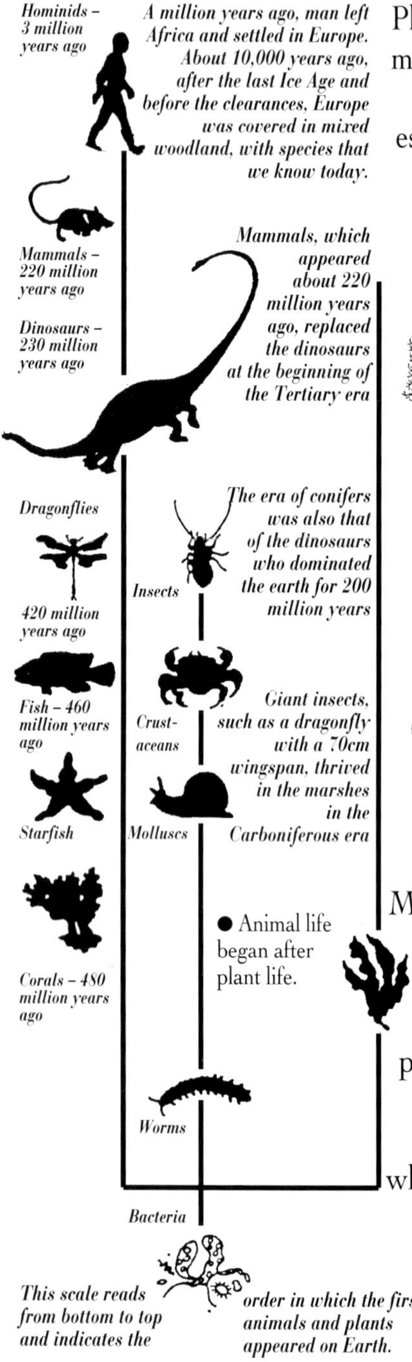

Millions of years later, plants with a vascular system capable of circulating water and sap appeared: plant life exploded on earth. Trees diversified: first into gymnosperms (conifers) when seeds evolved and then into angiosperms (broad-leaved trees) with the evolution of flowers with enclosed ovaries.

Hominids – 3 million years ago

A million years ago, man left Africa and settled in Europe. About 10,000 years ago, after the last Ice Age and before the clearances, Europe was covered in mixed woodland, with species that we know today.

Mammals – 220 million years ago

Dinosaurs – 230 million years ago

Mammals, which appeared about 220 million years ago, replaced the dinosaurs at the beginning of the Tertiary era

65 million years ago. At the beginning of the Tertiary era conifers began to decline and were gradually replaced by broad-leaved trees.

Dragonflies

The era of conifers was also that of the dinosaurs who dominated the earth for 200 million years

Insects

Between 200 and 130 million years ago. Land above sea level was dominated by conifers, the first true trees.

420 million years ago

Fish – 460 million years ago

Crustaceans

Giant insects, such as a dragonfly with a 70cm wingspan, thrived in the marshes in the Carboniferous era

Starfish

Molluscs

320 million years ago. In the Carboniferous period, land above sea level was marshy. The dominant plants were club mosses, horsetails and ferns, some of which were then more than 30m tall.

Corals – 480 million years ago

● Animal life began after plant life.

Worms

Bacteria

This scale reads from bottom to top and indicates the order in which the first animals and plants appeared on Earth.

42

● Romans built their villas in clearings, bringing many acres of land into cultivation, taking timber, fruit and game. Woodlands recovered following the great invasions.

● In the Middle Ages, as the population multiplied, clearing increased. Peasants extracted a wide range of products from the ever-shrinking woodland.

● During the 100 Years' War (towards the end of the Middle Ages) battles, as well as diseases, such as plague, reduced the population: the forest recovered.

● Until the 19th century, forests shrank, unable to meet the demands for wood. Replanting was ordered in an attempt to restore them.

● Vast plantations of conifers now cover parts of Europe, but they do not support the wide range of animal life found in natural woodlands.

Problems Facing Trees

Trees may suffer as a result of human activities which cause pollution, but also from natural disasters such as certain weather conditions (eg. storms and drought). In our time, the combination of these two factors is causing an alarming decline in trees.

- Several consecutive years of drought have left trees susceptible to disease and insect attack.

- Storms have destroyed poplar plantations: trees were either uprooted or their trunks snapped in half.

- In some eastern European countries the woodlands are very polluted. They receive all the toxic waste emitted by nearby factories.

- Tens of thousands of hectares are destroyed every year by fires. These start most easily in unmanaged bushy undergrowth.

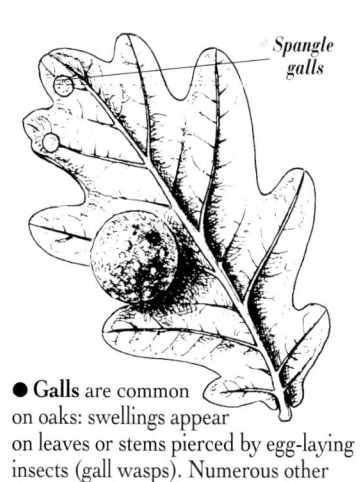

Spangle galls

For shelter, the processionary moth caterpillars construct large silken bags at the tips of branches

- **Galls** are common on oaks: swellings appear on leaves or stems pierced by egg-laying insects (gall wasps). Numerous other parasites attack and weaken trees.

- There have been attacks on trees by new predators: a fungus has been attacking plane trees in southern Europe since the 1970s, and the American bacteria which causes fire blight on apple trees is difficult to combat.

- The **caterpillar of the processionary moth** feeds on pine needles and can strip whole trees.

- Acid rain carries toxic waste which impoverishes the soil and weakens trees. We do not know the precise role played by acid rain in the decline of trees.

- The evergreen foliage of conifers is particularly sensitive to pollution.

- Fire can be prevented by woodland restoration and management.

- A healthy conifer has plump, green needles distributed all along the branches. When attacked by acid rain, drought, or disease, the leaves discolour and fall.

Glossary

- **ACUMINATE (LEAF)** Leaf ending in a long, drawn out point.

- **ALLUVIAL WOODLAND** Woodland in a valley bottom or beside a river.

- **ANTHER** The pollen sac at the tip of the stamen.

- **APPRESSED** Lying flat and close against a stem.

- **ARIL** A fleshy covering on a seed.

- **BERRY** A many-seeded, soft fleshy fruit.

- **BLADE** The flat part of a leaf.

- **BROAD-LEAVED TREE** A tree with flat leaves, as distinct from a conifer which has needles.

- **CALCAREOUS** Chalky.

- **CALYX** The usually green outer envelope or sepals of a flower.

- **CAMBIUM** Cells in the stem and roots of a plant which divide and make the stem or roots increase in girth.

- **CATKIN** Inflorescence arranged in a spike which is usually pendulous and flexible (willow, sweet chestnut).

- **CONE** Seed-bearing structure of a conifer composed of overlapping scales which protect the seed.

- **CONIFER** A tree with cones.

- **COMPOUND (LEAF)** Made up of several leaflets.

- **COPSE, COPPICE** A stand of broad-leaved trees that are periodically cut (coppiced) at the base. If some trees in a coppice are left uncut, these are called standards.

- **COROLLA** Inner floral envelope, composed of white or coloured petals.

- **CORYMB** A group of flowers with stalks arranged to form a flat-topped or domed inflorescence.

- **CUPULE** Cup-shaped structure, such as the cup around the base of an acorn.

- **DRUPE** A fleshy fruit with a single seed enclosed in a hard woody layer, the stone (eg. cherry).

- **EROSION** Loss of ground due to the action of water which washes away particles of soil.

- **EVERGREEN (LEAF)** A leaf which remains on the tree for several years: the opposite of a deciduous leaf which falls seasonally.

- **EXOTIC** A species imported from another country. The opposite of a native species.

- **FODDER** Food for livestock.

- **GARRIGUE** Low-growing shrubby vegetation, often spiny and strongly scented, characteristic of dry, alkaline soils in the Mediterranean area. Generally shorter than maquis.

- **GIRTH** The distance around the trunk of a tree.

- **HYBRIDISE** Hybridisation occurs when two different species are bred together.

- **INFLORESCENCE** A flower-head or flower cluster.

- **LAYING (HEDGE)** Hedge creation in which a young trunk is cut almost through and then laid almost horizontal. Shoots arise which grow into a dense hedge.

- **LANCEOLATE (LEAF)** A leaf shaped like a lance, narrowed at both ends.

- **LEAFLET** Separate division of a leaf.

- **LENTICEL** A pore through which the plant loses water.

- **LOBE** Part of a leaf, between two sinuses.